MANDY COLON

THE POWER OF STOICISM

Harnessing Ancient Wisdom for a Resilient Life
(2024 Guide for Beginners)

First edition

This book was professionally typeset on Reedsy.
Find out more at reedsy.com

Contents

1

INTRODUCTION

"Begin to embrace each day as a unique life, a complete entity in itself. Those who live this way, treating each day as a rounded whole, find tranquility in their minds." - Seneca.

Seneca narrated a story of an acquaintance who rose from poverty to success, but unfortunately passed away just as his hard work was bearing fruit. This made me realize the uncertainty of life, how we are bound by mortality, and how it is unwise to recklessly assume we have endless time to achieve grand plans. In the past, I used to make ambitious plans for the distant future at the start of each year, yet very few of those plans materialized.

However, I eventually grasped the importance of not just setting goals, but cultivating daily habits to attain them. Seneca suggested making grand plans for each quality day, understanding that if we live each day well and accumulate enough such days, we will ultimately lead a fulfilling life. This concept was truly eye-opening, but it didn't instantly transform my life. I remained discontented and dissatisfied, as the knowledge had not yet taken root in my actions.

In my youth, I observed people treating their ideas as mere accessories to their social image, superficial and devoid of genuine substance. Determined to seek deeper perspectives, I turned to reading old books. Among them, Marcus Aurelius' Meditations introduced me to philosophy and Stoicism, which profoundly impacted my life. Stoicism became my guiding principle, helping me gain control over my emotions, which previously influenced my decisions negatively.

Our minds hold a vast reservoir of information and experiences that shape our beliefs and values. Some of these beliefs may not be conducive to our well-being, yet we rarely question them or work to improve our lives intentionally. Embracing Stoicism involves bringing these beliefs to our conscious awareness, actively choosing what to believe and live by, and discarding unnecessary mental baggage.

Stoics such as Marcus Aurelius and Epictetus emphasized the power of our thoughts in shaping our experiences. Our minds act as lenses that color our perception of life; negative beliefs lead to suffering, while positive ones contribute to a good life. Fortunately, we have the ability to change our beliefs and, consequently, our experiences. Stoic philosophy provides practical and actionable strategies, readily available from its vast collection of wisdom, enabling us to lead a good life regardless of the circumstances. It focuses on what truly matters and empowers us to strengthen our character and find peace within ourselves.

2

HOW TO BE A STOIC LIKE EPICTETUS - WHAT CAN YOU CONTROL?

Becoming a Stoic like Epictetus involves understanding what is within our control and what is not, gradually applying rational, practical wisdom to distressing situations. Stoicism advocates cultivating a virtuous and rational mindset, being in harmony with nature, and maintaining indifference toward external circumstances. This ancient philosophy traces its roots back to Zeno in 300 BC, and one of the traditional approaches is exemplified by Epictetus and his three disciplines: desire, action, and assent.

Epictetus, born as a slave in Hierapolis around 55 AD, had a profound impact on my life during a challenging period marked by a troubled long-distance relationship and disillusionment with politics. His teachings offered solace by emphasizing that only our judgments about right and wrong are entirely within our control. Desire for things like reputation, sex, health, or wealth, which lie outside our control, leads to unhappiness and frustration. While we cannot avoid human flashes of desire or fear, being Stoic entails examining them to determine if they relate to uncontrollable factors. If so, we must respond with the understanding that they are not our concern.

Reflecting on our anxieties, we realize that much of our pain stems not from actual misfortunes but from the shame we feel for things beyond our control. Epictetus was once a slave of Epaphroditus but pursued education and philosophy under Musonius Rufus after gaining freedom. He continued teaching philosophy throughout his life, despite facing challenging political circumstances. His unwavering focus on what was within his control kept him going, symbolized by his earthenware lamp, which he cherished and learned a valuable lesson from after it was stolen: a man loses only what he already possesses.

Epictetus' enduring wisdom provides a framework for navigating life's troubles, exemplified by his own struggles with a disabled leg, a likely result of abuse during his time as a slave. He believed that sickness might affect the body but not one's ability to make decisions. Stoicism offers a profound way to approach life, providing guidance on how to face adversity with strength and resilience.

EPICTETUS' PERSPECTIVE ON THE MODERN WORLD

Whenever you encounter difficulties, whether it's illness or obstacles in your plans, remember that these challenges only impede your progress if you allow them to do so.

Epictetus' work, "The Enchiridion," begins with a fundamental principle that has become a cornerstone of stoic philosophy. He asks a crucial question: What falls within your sphere of control? According to Epictetus, it is virtuous to desire only what you have the power to influence. Refrain from getting upset or angry over things beyond your control, such as external events or others' actions. Instead, focus on your own behavior. This mindset will enable you to let go of unnecessary burdens and accept the present reality while empowering you to take charge of what lies within your grasp. As Epictetus stated, we can control our opinions, desires, aversions, and actions, but we cannot dictate our possessions, reputation, physical body, or other people's behaviors.

To be a stoic like Epictetus, emulate real leaders who demonstrate their wisdom through actions rather than mere words. Set a standard for yourself and embody it through your choices and actions, rather than merely talking about it. Invest your time and energy in living up to your standards. Following Epictetus' example, never settle for theoretical ideas that do not shape your actual conduct.

Epictetus recognized that much of our behavior stems from habitual patterns, and he encouraged his students to establish principles and standards to guide their lives. If you are starting your journey with stoicism, this approach can be challenging but fruitful. Create a character for yourself and take small steps each day towards becoming the person you aspire to be. In the context of this book, this character means adopting a commitment to apply tried and tested stoic wisdom in moments of distress.

By following these three steps, you can begin integrating stoicism into your life, allowing the grapevine of your virtues to blossom and bear fruit. We have learned so far that life inevitably presents circumstances beyond our control, but we become most effective when we focus only on what we can control. Establishing a standard and character will keep you on the right path.

In the next chapter, we will delve into the three pillars of stoicism, providing you with a deeper understanding of the commitment you are making to this philosophy.

3

THE THREE PILLARS OF STOICISM EXPLAINED - EMBRACING VIRTUE

Athenaeus the Epigrammatist, as quoted by Diogenes, extolled the wisdom of the Stoic teachings, which advocate that virtue is the only true good. Virtue safeguards human lives and societies more effectively than walls and gates can. Stoicism encompasses three fundamental areas: ethics, physics, and logic, as elucidated by Zeno the Citium, the philosophy's founder.

Physics, in the Stoic sense, refers to understanding the universe's divine and natural aspects. The Stoics perceived the cosmos as a divine entity, underpinned by reason or logos. Logic, the second pillar, involves how we think about the world, both as individuals and as a society. The Stoics believed that logic was integral to the fabric of the universe and that God represented the creative and productive aspect of this cosmic unfolding.

While much emphasis is placed on the practical aspects of Stoicism, particularly ethics, the philosophy also delves into understanding logic and physics. Logic serves as the foundational art of Stoicism, guiding one's thinking and providing a solid framework for comprehending the other pillars.

Stoic logic follows certain rules of language, much like the example of asserting that it is light outside when looking out of a window during the day. Such rules govern the world and form the basis of logos, which represents natural principles of existence.

Ethics, the third pillar, revolves around discerning appropriate actions from inappropriate ones. Once logic is mastered, the Stoics believed individuals could delve into ethics, dividing it into virtue and vice. Virtue leads to happiness, while vice results in misery. Additionally, there exists a gray area of morally neutral actions or indifferents.

Indifferents are context-dependent actions that are neither inherently good nor bad. The key lies in reasoning to determine how to use these indifferents, as it is their application that affects happiness. The Stoics considered life as part of the interconnected system called "nature." A good life harmonizes with nature, aligning with virtue, while vice opposes nature.

Within indifferents, there are preferred and dispreferred ones. Preferred indifferents, like strength, pleasure, and wealth, have a positive impact on our natural condition but do not guarantee happiness. On the other hand, dispreferred indifferents, such as poverty, weakness, and disease, slightly worsen our natural condition but only cause misery if we allow them to do so. How we utilize these indifferents ultimately determines whether we lead a content and happy life.

THE FOUNDATION OF STOICISM: EMBRACING THE UNIVERSE

Understanding and living in harmony with nature form the essence of Stoicism. When Stoics referred to physics, they meant comprehending the universe, not the modern scientific field. Their understanding of the universe was intricate, but the basics can be introduced. They believed in the divine entity called the logos, the force behind reason. Within this universe, there exist two levels – pneuma and matter. Matter encompasses all that we perceive with our senses; it is lifeless, destructible, and passive. On the other hand, pneuma is the active force propelling the cosmos. It is inseparable from matter and indestructible, often seen as the vehicle for the logos. Pneuma gives life to the universe, driving the movements of celestial bodies and even life itself. Stoics held the view that life's outcomes are predetermined, with multiple realities, and your choices determine the reality you experience.

The three pillars of Stoicism – physics, ethics, and logic – are interdependent. Some scholars likened their interaction to an egg, where physics is the yolk, ethics is the egg white, and logic is the shell. They argued that understanding how the universe works is essential in determining what is good or bad. Pursuing virtue is at the heart of Stoicism; according to the Stoics, it is the only true good in life. Virtue entails living in harmony with nature, which they considered divine. Committing to the pursuit of virtue is the key to attaining happiness.

Discipline is crucial in this pursuit, as it serves as the foundation for Stoic philosophy. It keeps individuals progressing towards their goals. To recap,

Stoicism is a philosophical system built on the pillars of logic, physics, and ethics, with each pillar supporting the others. Logic guides our thinking, ethics directs our practical actions according to the divine, and physics explores the divine universe. Pursuing virtue leads to happiness in the Stoic worldview.

4

MARCUS AURELIUS AND THE POWER OF SELF-DISCIPLINE - EMBRACING FREEDOM THROUGH DISCIPLINED LIVING

In our current era, many individuals grapple with uncertainty, fear, and doubt. The prevalent question on everyone's mind is, "How can I find the strength to persevere?" When facing tough times, it might feel as though the world has come to an end, but life never truly halts. So, what should one do in such situations? Can a crisis lead to personal growth and improvement? The stoics resoundingly answer, "Yes," but with a crucial caveat - it requires the right mindset. A crisis can indeed be a transformative teacher, guiding individuals to let go of the past, trust their instincts, build resilience, learn forgiveness, and glean various valuable lessons. However, why do so many people go through crises without learning and evolving?

The answer lies in self-discipline, or rather, the lack thereof. Without self-discipline, personal achievements, goals, and success remain elusive. Many embark on endeavors lacking the determination to see them through, inevitably shifting focus to something else when faced with adversity, only to repeat the cycle. Self-discipline stands as the paramount attribute essential for achieving excellence, a practical philosophy embraced by the Stoics. In this chapter, we delve into the essence of discipline, the obstacles impeding its cultivation, and insights gleaned from Marcus Aurelius on fostering this transformative virtue.

So, what exactly is self-discipline? It is the ability to persist, push oneself, and stay steadfast despite the emotions and challenges one encounters. Although highly sought after, self-discipline has become increasingly difficult to develop in our modern world. The prevalence of "habit-changing" months, like No Nut November, Stoptober, or Dry January, indicates a genuine desire to adopt positive habits and self-discipline. Yet, altering habits remains a challenging endeavor.

How many times have you set goals or crafted plans with the promise of doing things differently, only to abandon them after a few days? How often have your impulses led you back to your old habits despite your best intentions? Discipline necessitates overcoming short-term desires, be it in pursuing business ventures, spending quality time with family, or attaining fitness goals. It demands resisting the allure of snacking, indulging in movies, or other temptations.

Discipline does not imply that temptations vanish with increased self-discipline; they will persist. However, self-discipline grants the strength to resist such impulses. The more one resists and exercises discipline, the stronger it becomes, akin to a muscle's growth with consistent training. It is important to differentiate discipline from motivation. While motivation may help initiate action, it can be inconsistent and fleeting. Relying solely on motivation often leads to procrastination or a relapse into old habits. In contrast, discipline is steadfast and propels individuals forward, even during times of wavering motivation. In essence, discipline is true freedom.

THE CHALLENGES OF CULTIVATING SELF-DISCIPLINE

Developing self-discipline is no simple feat; it's akin to ascending an endless mountain with no peak in sight. Two significant obstacles make the journey even more arduous:

Temptation:

Our surroundings are inundated with distractions and alluring temptations, making it increasingly difficult to resist impulsive behaviors. Platforms like YouTube, video games, and social media are designed to captivate our attention and keep us hooked. This constant noise presents a formidable challenge to achieving self-discipline, but it should not serve as an excuse.

Zero resistance:

The ease and convenience prevailing in today's world hinder the development of discipline. With services like Amazon's next-day delivery, quick food orders, instant gratification from social media, and limitless entertainment on platforms like Netflix, opportunities for discipline are dwindling. Instant rewards are gradually shaping us into impatient individuals with short attention spans. The quest for comfort is reducing our sources of resistance, which is essential for discipline to flourish. Too much ease becomes a trap, depriving us of growth opportunities.

Building Self-Discipline with Marcus Aurelius

Marcus Aurelius, one of history's influential figures, offered profound insights into self-discipline, the very essence of Stoicism. Despite holding immense power during his reign, he found time to pen his thoughts in "Meditations." The following wisdom from Marcus Aurelius can aid in developing self-discipline:

Find your purpose:

According to Marcus Aurelius, everyone has a unique purpose, and our moral duty is to discover and fulfill it. Understanding our goals and how each daily task contributes to those goals empowers us to maintain self-discipline.

Knowing our "why" becomes a significant source of motivation, propelling us forward even when we are unsure of what to do. The key is to start and keep doing it because we are meant to.

Trust in yourself:

Marcus Aurelius advises making our desires a solid foundation and keeping our minds centered on our purpose. Once we identify our purpose, we must devise a practical action plan to reach our goals. Committing not only to the overarching goal but also to the small daily actions helps maintain focus and discipline. Regardless of our emotional, mental, or physical state, self-discipline keeps us on track.

Creating an action plan built on achievable milestones provides a sense of control and prevents feeling overwhelmed. This approach helps avoid procrastination, a roadblock to self-discipline, as it leads to digression or stagnation. Only by overcoming these challenges can we genuinely claim to possess self-discipline.

NURTURING SELF-DISCIPLINE: LESSONS FROM MARCUS AURELIUS

Marcus Aurelius emphasized the significance of everyday actions in shaping our lives. Being satisfied with each daily action's best achievement is essential for building discipline. It requires consistency, showing up every day, and putting in the work. Self-discipline becomes a habit that grows stronger with practice.

Voluntary exposure to hardship is another valuable lesson from Marcus Aurelius. In a world of convenience, embracing challenges willingly toughens us for greater trials. Engaging in voluntary hardships, such as cold showers or abstaining from vices, helps us realize that we can live without some comforts.

Avoid victimizing yourself, Marcus Aurelius urged. Refrain from making excuses like "I was born this way" or "I was never taught better." Take responsibility for your actions and be proactive. Adopt an empowering perspective, reframing challenges as opportunities for growth and improvement.

Delay gratification is a crucial aspect of self-discipline. Human beings must align with nature's demands and resist immediate desires to achieve long-term goals. It involves sacrificing instant pleasures for greater future rewards.

Marcus Aurelius advised ignoring critics, recognizing that their negativity often reflects their own insecurities. Don't waste energy on naysayers. Seek feedback from respected sources and ignore the rest.

Self-awareness is pivotal for self-discipline. Regularly review your days, identifying weaknesses and formulating strategies for improvement. Embrace introspection without self-judgment and commit to doing better each day.

Marcus Aurelius saw stoicism as a soothing remedy for life's challenges. It involves mastering impulses and building discipline like a muscle through resistance. His teachings, including delayed gratification, ignoring naysayers, and consistent effort, guide the path to self-discipline.

In the upcoming chapter, we will explore how to apply stoicism to enrich our lives. Drawing from Epictetus' metaphors for life, we will uncover the wisdom to lead a happy and virtuous life.

5

EPICTETUS' GUIDANCE FOR LIFE - THE IMPACT OF ATTITUDE

"Do you intend to wait long before demanding the best for yourself?" – *Epictetus.*

It is a common belief that our attitude plays a crucial role in life. Our attitude influences our actions, and having the right attitude leads to positive outcomes. No amount of handshakes and smiles will suffice if our attitude is misguided. However, little has been said about precisely what constitutes the right attitude and how to attain it. How can we live the best life possible and effectively handle life's challenges? How can we thrive? The stoic attitude holds the key. It involves comprehending that the actions of others are not our responsibility or burden. Each one of us is accountable for our daily thoughts and deeds.

EPICTETUS' METAPHORS FOR LIFE – EMBRACING THE STOIC ATTITUDE

Epictetus employed various metaphors to elucidate the importance of attitude in life. In this exploration, we'll delve into these metaphors to internalize and adopt the stoic attitude for our own lives.

Life is a festival:

Epictetus likened life to a grand festival orchestrated by God. By perceiving life in this way, we find joy in its experiences. Enduring hardships becomes more manageable when we focus on the bigger picture and recognize our role in the grand play orchestrated by the divine. Epictetus encourages us to discover our purpose, recognizing that our mortality is an opportunity to participate in this divine festival and fulfill our duty as citizens of God's great city.

Life is a game:

Drawing inspiration from dice games, Epictetus teaches that in life, external circumstances carry no inherent moral charge. The essence lies in how we play the game. Similarly, in a ball game, the ball itself holds no good or bad value; what matters is the players' skill, judgment, and dexterity. By understanding life as a game, we are called to actively engage and participate, taking responsibility for our actions and choices.

Life is like weaving:

Drawing a connection between life as a game and life as weaving, Epictetus compares the use of wool in weaving to the role of the ball in the game metaphor. In both instances, it is our duty to utilize our resources wisely and create the best outcome possible.

Life is a play:

Epictetus views life as a theatrical play where we are the actors. Although we aim to play specific roles, we must accept that fate determines the roles assigned to us. Embracing this metaphor, we understand that we are not the authors of the play; rather, we act within the script provided by a higher power. Our task is to perform our roles to the best of our abilities, regardless of their nature.

Life is an athletic contest:

Similar to athletes preparing for competition, Epictetus sees the study of stoic ethics as our preparation for flourishing in life. He urges us not to delay taking action in life due to perceived lack of preparation. Just as an athlete cannot wait indefinitely for ideal conditions to train, we must actively participate in life, making progress despite challenges.

Life is military service:

Epictetus teaches that everyone serves God, whether they realize it or not. By comparing life to military service, he emphasizes the importance of fulfilling our responsibilities diligently. Like soldiers who must carry out their orders, we, too, should strive to serve to the best of our abilities without complaining or shirking our duties.

In understanding and embracing these metaphors, we can cultivate the stoic attitude, leading to a more purposeful and fulfilling life. In the following chapter, we will explore the stoics' beliefs regarding virtue, its pursuit, and its role in achieving happiness.

How do you perceive your life?

What kind of attitude do you carry with you as you journey through life? Are you neglecting to savor life's joys, fulfill your responsibilities, or actively engage in the challenges it presents? In this section, we have discovered that:

- Life is like a festival, meant to be enjoyed.
- Life resembles a game, and in this game, you must skillfully weave your actions to achieve the best outcome.
- Life is akin to a theatrical play, and it is your responsibility to perform your role well.
- Life can be compared to an athletic contest, where your active participation is essential.
- Life is akin to military service, and it calls for the dutiful fulfillment of your responsibilities.

In the upcoming chapter, we will delve into the stoics' beliefs regarding virtue. As happiness is intrinsically linked to the pursuit of virtue, we will explore how to embrace virtue and understand its significance.

6

UNDERSTANDING STOIC VIRTUE - THE ULTIMATE GOOD

"If it is not right, do not do it. If it is not true, do not say it." – *Marcus Aurelius.*

The concept of "the highest good" was coined by Cicero, one of Rome's greatest orators. It refers to the ultimate goal we should strive for in life. For the stoics, this highest good is virtue. They believed that no matter what challenges life throws at us, every situation presents an opportunity for a virtuous response. Even in the face of fear and pain, the stoics emphasized the importance of responding with virtue. They asserted that happiness, reputation, success, love, and honor follow when we act virtuously. Thus, a person possessing virtue has everything they need to lead a fulfilling life. But what exactly did the stoics mean by virtue? In this section, we will delve deeper into their understanding of virtue and apply it to our own lives. According to the stoics, there are four primary virtues: wisdom, temperance, courage, and justice.

UNDERSTANDING STOIC VIRTUES

Wisdom:

Epictetus emphasized that the main objective in life is to gain self-awareness and discern the things we can and cannot control. He argued that good and evil do not lie in external circumstances but rather in our choices. True wisdom lies in understanding this and making virtuous decisions. Diogenes further defined wisdom as the ability to distinguish between what is good, what is evil, and what is neither. It involves knowing what to choose, what to fear, and what to remain indifferent to. Once this knowledge is acquired, our actions naturally align with wisdom.

Temperance:

Marcus Aurelius discussed tranquility and advocated doing only what is necessary to achieve peace in life. To live in peace means to engage in activities essential for our social existence as and when they arise. It also means eliminating what is non-essential. He advised his students to constantly question themselves: "Is this necessary?" Aristotle shared a similar concept, which he called the "golden mean." He argued that virtue lies between deficiency and excess. Excessive behaviors lead to dissatisfaction, while temperance promotes contentment and self-control. In other words, knowing when enough is enough and not relying on pleasure for happiness are integral aspects of temperance.

Courage:

Epictetus compared life to military service, where each individual plays a crucial role in the ongoing battle. Life is unpredictable and challenging, and your position in this "battlefield" is significant throughout your lifetime. Epictetus urged people to thrive by resisting and persisting. Courage has always been an essential virtue in stoic philosophy, exemplified by individuals who display unwavering bravery, even in hopeless situations. To the stoics, courage meant standing up against misfortune, upholding principles despite inconvenience, and living by one's truth.

Justice:

Marcus Aurelius believed that justice should be present in every action we undertake. Every just act serves the common good. Among the four stoic virtues, Marcus Aurelius considered justice the most significant, as it gives birth to the other virtues. Justice, according to Cicero, is the crown jewel of virtues. It extends beyond merely legal aspects and encompasses our duties and interactions with others. Justice governs societal bonds and fosters a harmonious community, promoting the idea that no one should harm others or infringe on private property while acknowledging shared resources. Justice also implies that we exist for others, and we are interconnected with the world. Epictetus highlighted that expecting the best from ourselves means genuinely caring for others, further reinforcing the notion that honoring equality and working for the greater good is the noblest path one can take.

In conclusion, stoic virtue encompasses wisdom, temperance, courage, and justice, forming the foundation for leading a fulfilling and principled life.

What is your approach to life?

To live a life of freedom and happiness, virtue is indispensable. Luckily, the concept of virtue is neither obscure nor extravagant in the eyes of the stoics. They shunned complex ideas that lacked practicality. In essence, stoic virtue can be summarized as follows: a stoic believes that they can only control their response to the world, and that response should be characterized by courage, justice, wisdom, and temperance. Life is inherently unpredictable, and many aspects are beyond our control. This realization could either overwhelm and immobilize us or liberate us. As we explored in this chapter:

Virtue is the key to finding freedom in acknowledging the aspects of life beyond our control.

A virtuous person knows that, regardless of circumstances, they possess the power of reason and choice. They are committed to doing what is right, guided by virtue.

Virtue is the only aspect within our control, and by embracing it, everything else falls into place.

How do you approach life? Do you confront challenges with temperance, wisdom, courage, and justice? In the subsequent chapter, we will delve into the teachings of another stoic philosopher, Seneca, and his insights on making the most of the time we have in this theatrical performance called life.

7

SENECA'S TIME MANAGEMENT STRATEGIES

"Procrastination wastes our life by stealing each day as it comes and promising a future that may never arrive." – Lucius Annaeus Seneca.

Time management challenges are a common aspect of our lives, especially in the workplace. We often start our days with high hopes of meeting deadlines, engaging in self-care, and accomplishing tasks, only to be sidetracked by unexpected events. However, Seneca's wisdom can help us regain control over our time.

Lucius Annaeus Seneca, a Roman stoic philosopher and statesman, faced both triumphs and tribulations throughout his life. Despite experiencing sorrow and controversy, he remained committed to his stoic beliefs even when facing a threat of death. Seneca's enduring influence can still be felt today through his writings, where he offers valuable insights on various life aspects, including time management.

To make the most of our time, Seneca advises us to treat it as our most precious resource. While many perceive time as fleeting, Seneca argues that it is abundant if used wisely. He suggests auditing our daily activities for a week to understand how we spend our time. This audit helps identify unproductive habits, reveal peak productivity periods, and set realistic daily goals.

One crucial aspect of effective time management is creating a schedule or a to-do list for each day. Having a plan on paper alleviates anxiety about unaccomplished tasks. Moreover, our subconscious processes these plans while we sleep, leading to fresh insights upon waking up.

Seneca acknowledges the challenges of adhering to schedules. To combat procrastination caused by the conflict between short-term rewards and long-term goals, known as "present bias," he proposes immediate rewards for each goal. By intertwining short-term gratification with long-term aspirations, we can overcome the struggle between our present and future selves. For instance, if we aim to exercise regularly but enjoy socializing, joining a sports team allows us to achieve both goals simultaneously.

Adopting Seneca's strategies empowers us to manage our time efficiently, embrace productivity, and enrich our lives with meaningful accomplishments.

Optimize Your Time Wisely

A key element in managing your time effectively is setting limits on task durations rather than striving to complete them in one go. Taking short breaks between tasks can balance focus and rest, reducing mental strain and maintaining motivation. Once you finish the allotted time for a task, move on to the next priority. You'll notice your productivity increase and your to-do list shrink.

However, it's crucial not to be overly ambitious. Seneca warns against obsessively pursuing achievements and goals, which can lead to misery and a shortened life. Living solely for achievements disregards the fleeting nature of time and creates an endless cycle of discontent. In a consumerist culture that promotes constant striving, limiting your tasks will help you reconnect with your purpose and avoid falling into the trap of consumerism.

Reflect on Mortality

We often squander time because we forget that life is finite, and no one escapes death. We act as if we have all the time in the world, unaware of the precious moments slipping away. Contemplating mortality can profoundly influence our lives. If we view death as distant, we may take our days for granted and waste them. By acknowledging the reality of death, we can stop deferring happiness to an imaginary future and embrace the present.

By embracing the inevitability of death, we can avoid wasting time on futile planning. Seneca warns against constant preoccupation with the future, urging us to live each day as if it were our last. Considering our mortality can liberate us from the tyranny of procrastination and help us appreciate the significance of the present moment.

Embrace Single-Tasking

A simple yet effective time management strategy is to avoid multitasking and focus on one task at a time. Eliminate distractions and resist the allure of busyness. Multitasking may seem appealing, but it often leads to decreased productivity and wasted time. Avoid falling into the busyness trap, which falsely glorifies constant activity. Instead, seek solitude and genuine reflection to increase your productivity.

Ultimately, time is your most precious and irreplaceable resource. Contemplating mortality can shape how you live your life and empower you to make the most of each day. Say goodbye to multitasking and embrace single-tasking to achieve greater productivity and focus. By incorporating these principles into your daily routine, you'll find yourself living more intentionally and making the most of your time in this fleeting existence.

8

DISTURBING FACTORS TO INNER PEACE

In the previous chapter, we discussed the significance of being able to sit quietly by yourself in a room, free from turmoil. However, many people are unfamiliar with the tranquility of inner peace, as their minds are often filled with turbulence. The stoics greatly emphasized the pursuit of inner peace, and in this section, we will explore the obstacles that hinder its attainment. Understanding these hindrances will empower you to work on eliminating them.

The Thirst for Validation

Seeking validation from others is a futile endeavor, as we cannot control their opinions of us. No matter how much effort we put into impressing others, their approval remains beyond our reach. Some individuals may dislike us for reasons beyond our control, and that's simply a part of life. To achieve inner peace, we must accept that the pursuit of external validation is weak and fruitless. As Epictetus wisely stated, true virtue lies in focusing on what we can control, and our happiness should not be subject to the judgments of others.

Anxiety Over the Past and Future

Our minds cannot find peace if we cling to the past or constantly worry about the future. Dwelling on past events burdens us, yet we cannot alter what has already occurred. Moreover, our memory is unreliable, often distorted by biases. Instead, we should extract valuable lessons from our past experiences and let go of the events themselves. Embracing the transient nature of time, as Marcus Aurelius described, allows us to flow along the river of life without getting trapped in the past or fixating on a predetermined future.

The Perfectionism Trap

Perfectionists endure constant anxiety as they relentlessly pursue an unattainable ideal. They are never satisfied with their achievements, as their desire for flawlessness renders every result inadequate. Rather than seeking perfection, we should strive for excellence, which is a realistic and achievable goal. Pursuing excellence allows us to embrace our imperfections and find contentment in continual growth.

The Fear of Aging and Death

Some individuals fear aging and death, obsessively trying to stall the inevitable process. While adopting a healthy lifestyle can extend one's lifespan, aging remains an unavoidable part of life. Fearing the inevitable causes undue anxiety and prevents us from accepting the natural course of existence.

The Fear of the Unknown

Another group of people fears the unknown, leading to unnecessary apprehension about new experiences or unfamiliar cultures. While being cautious in novel situations is natural, excessive fear of the unknown can create irrational anxieties and fantasies about imagined scenarios. This fear disrupts our inner peace and undermines our trust in the unfolding of life.

Identifying Disturbing Factors

Anything that disrupts our inner peace does so by triggering negative emotions such as anxiety, frustration, anger, or stress. These emotions alter our perception of reality and compel us to act irrationally. Ultimately, we expend valuable energy and time on matters beyond our control. The stoics offered a way to address these powerful emotions, which we will explore later. Before doing so, let's recap what we've learned:

The fear of the future, death, the desire for validation, and other factors can disturb our inner peace when we allow them to.

Disturbances to inner peace arise from our inability to control our internal narrative and manage our emotions effectively.

We cannot control external circumstances, and there is no guarantee that our fears won't materialize. However, we can empower ourselves to respond rationally and confidently by embracing the wisdom of the stoics.

9

MAINTAINING CALM: EPICTETUS' APPROACH

Encounters with frustrations are inevitable in our daily lives. Often, things don't unfold as we desire, and bad news may upset our plans. Attempting to control everything becomes futile, leading to diminishing expectations and recurring frustrations. To break this cycle and make better decisions amid challenges, we can learn valuable lessons from Epictetus' wisdom on maintaining calm.

Reevaluate Your Notion of the 'Self'

Epictetus had a unique perspective on the 'self,' distinct from the common beliefs held by most individuals. Unlike many who tie their identity to reputation, status, and possessions, Epictetus viewed the 'self' differently. He found true empowerment by disassociating his 'self' from external circumstances. Even as a slave, he believed that his will was invincible, beyond the physical constraints imposed upon him. Understanding that our bodies and external possessions are not truly ours liberates us, ensuring that our inner peace remains intact.

Practice Intentions

To retain calm when it matters most, Epictetus advises rehearsing our intentions. In situations where numerous factors lie beyond our control, aligning our intentions with nature becomes crucial. Deciding in advance to act rationally, in line with our reasoning abilities, allows us to navigate through challenges with wisdom. Epictetus exemplified this by preparing himself mentally before visiting public baths, deciding to maintain composure even if his possessions were stolen. By setting intentions, we retain the freedom to exercise reason and respond thoughtfully to circumstances.

Pause and Assess

When faced with difficulties, Epictetus posed a critical question: "What is out of my control?" To regain control over our emotions, we must learn to pause and ponder this question. In moments of emotional turbulence, we often overlook how little control we truly have. By mastering the art of pausing and reflecting, we can strip away irrelevant concerns and focus on what lies within our realm of influence. This clarity enables us to direct our will and govern our impressions of the world.

Choose the Path Forward

Gaining perspective through a pause is valuable, but it remains futile unless we channel it into our actions. Once we identify what we can control, the next step is to decide how to exert that control. Despite enduring a life of slavery, Epictetus defied the dehumanization and loss of identity by asserting control over his responses to controllable circumstances. This empowerment allowed him to shape his destiny and maintain inner composure amid adversity.

Embrace Calmness in Adversity

As we navigate life's trials, we often encounter temptations to succumb to sadness, frustration, or irritation. However, Epictetus taught us valuable lessons in this chapter:

Our response to events is within our control.

By setting intentions in advance, we can preserve our composure.

Taking a pause in the midst of turmoil is always beneficial.

By applying Epictetus' teachings, we can cultivate inner calm and face frustrations with a rational and composed demeanor.

10

MANAGING ANGER INSPIRED BY SENECA

Seneca offered valuable insights on anger management, emphasizing the need to eradicate anger entirely rather than merely controlling it. To adopt his approach, here are five effective ways to handle anger:

Recognize Anger's Destructive Nature

Seneca firmly believed that anger holds no utility and hampers sound judgment. By acknowledging its potential to hinder rationality, we can steer clear of falling into its grip. Unlike Aristotle, who deemed anger justifiable in certain contexts, Seneca advocated for complete avoidance of anger, considering it unreasonable and detrimental. By understanding anger's destructive essence, we can take the first step towards handling it wisely.

Identify Your Triggers

Each individual faces unique triggers that provoke anger more intensely than others. Seneca suggested addressing these triggers as soon as they surface by maintaining composure and suppressing the emotion. Being mindful of our triggers empowers us to recognize the warning signs of anger, allowing us to prevent its escalation in a timely manner. Some common triggers include mistreatment by others, witnessing injustices, facing rejection, experiencing prejudice, and more. Awareness of these triggers enables us to respond more effectively.

Pause and Reflect

Seneca advocated for the practice of pausing before reacting to anger. This pause allows the initial passion of anger to subside, clearing the fog in our minds, and enabling a clearer perspective. This space between the stimulus and response allows for better decision-making, as anger impairs problem-solving abilities. By restraining ourselves from immediate retaliation and seeking peace before responding, we avoid making regrettable choices.

Harness the Power of Art

For those prone to anger, Seneca advised avoiding demanding tasks and pursuing pleasurable arts instead. Engaging in activities like reading poetry, listening to music, or exploring stories can calm the mind and foster inner peace. This approach, known as "expressive theory" in psychology, encourages releasing pent-up anger through creative outlets. Art therapy can be beneficial in healing unresolved anger and stabilizing emotions.

Empathize with Others

Putting ourselves in the shoes of those who anger us can offer valuable perspective. Seneca urged his students to contemplate how they might behave in similar circumstances and reflect on their own past actions. This exercise helps us recognize the fallacy in our self-worth estimation and our reluctance to accept treatment we would dish out to others. By empathizing with the offender, we gain a more comprehensive understanding of the situation and can temper our own reactions.

Conclusion

Dealing with anger requires self-awareness and a commitment to better managing our emotions. By adopting Seneca's wisdom, we can embrace a path of thoughtful introspection, recognizing anger's destructive nature, identifying triggers, pausing before responding, utilizing art for soothing, and practicing empathy. Let us strive to heal and find inner peace, recognizing that anger's bitterness should never outlast our capacity for understanding and forgiveness.

11

EMBRACING AMOR FATI - CONQUERING ANXIETY

Seneca once questioned the usefulness of burdening ourselves with bemoaning troubles, and this sentiment holds true when it comes to anxiety. Worrying excessively about the future can lead to short-term or long-term anxiety, leaving us feeling disempowered. However, the stoics introduced a powerful remedy known as "Amor Fati" - the love of fate. This concept encourages embracing whatever life brings our way with strength and resilience.

Amor Fati is the mindset of making the best out of every situation, treating each moment as an opportunity for growth rather than avoidance. It involves accepting that life's events are recurring infinitely, and we have the power to respond to them with love and determination. This mentality is not about passivity; it is about actively pursuing our goals while gracefully accepting the outcome, whether it aligns with our desires or not.

In the face of life-altering changes, the anxious version of ourselves may be consumed by worry and uncertainty, judging each outcome as either favorable or unfavorable. However, the stoic approach reminds us that life continues, and we only have the present moment in our grasp - neither the past nor the future.

By focusing on the present, we can better navigate life's challenges and uncertainties. The stoic way urges us to embrace our fate, working diligently towards our goals while understanding that external factors may influence the outcomes. Amor Fati empowers us to accept and adapt to whatever life presents, finding meaning and purpose regardless of the circumstances.

Anxiety need not be a destructive force in our lives. Embracing Amor Fati ensures that we remain on the right path, alleviating unnecessary worries and preserving our energy for more meaningful pursuits. By reminding ourselves that life goes on, staying rooted in the present, and embracing our destiny wholeheartedly, we can conquer anxiety and discover the inner peace and strength that lie within us.

12

FREEING YOURSELF FROM UNNECESSARY WORRIES - SENECA'S WISDOM

Seneca once wisely noted that our imagination can be more terrifying than reality itself. Many of us are prone to worry, and often, our anxieties stem from incessantly dwelling on the future and its countless possibilities. However, the future is not yet real, and we cannot live in its uncertainty. So, how can we deal with worry in the stoic way?

Firstly, it is crucial to ground ourselves in the present and acknowledge that worry is a deceptive liar, creating illusions about what is yet to come. The future is an abstract concept, and our focus should remain on the tangible reality of the present moment.

When faced with groundless fears of the future, we must recognize that we cannot predict or control every circumstance. Trying to prepare for every eventuality is akin to shooting in the dark. Instead, we should face these ideas, discern truth from speculation, and let go of unfounded worries.

To fortify our minds against worrisome thoughts, Seneca advised embracing the truth about the unpredictable nature of fortune and misfortune. Misfortunes will come and go, but they cannot be accurately foreseen. By guarding our minds against undue influences and acknowledging the fickleness of fortune, we can protect ourselves from unnecessary suffering.

Moreover, we should remember that bad fortune is transient. Life's challenges may come unexpectedly, but they do not stay forever. Just as the Buddhist man found an unexpected escape from a perilous situation, our hardships, too, shall pass.

Dealing with worry does not imply turning a blind eye to potential adversities. Seneca encouraged us to observe with care, avoiding both ignorance and obsession. Mindful assessment of situations and keeping our options open allow us to navigate life's uncertainties with resilience.

In summary, worry can be detrimental to our well-being, often based on false judgments and groundless fears. To overcome worry in the stoic way, we should anchor ourselves in reality, discern truth from illusion, observe the future mindfully, and remind ourselves of the ever-changing nature of fortune. By doing so, we can free ourselves from unnecessary worries and embrace a more content and serene existence.

13

MASTERING SELF-CONTROL - EMBRACING STOIC WISDOM

Seneca and the stoics emphasized the importance of self-control. By exercising restraint, one can avoid acting on impulses and addictive behaviors, remaining focused on what truly matters. The stoics' distinction between what we can and cannot control emphasizes the significance of focusing on self-control.

Self-controlled individuals are less swayed by external approval, temptations, or triggers. They can free themselves from unnecessary worries and anxieties, discerning between genuine needs and imagined desires. Developing self-control is a valuable journey, and the stoics offer practical advice on how to achieve it.

To cultivate self-control, Seneca suggested abstaining from something you love for a few days. By detaching ourselves from luxuries occasionally, we can test our minds and demystify any fears associated with deprivation. This could range from abstaining from social media to limiting smartphone use.

Marcus Aurelius proposed limiting leisure time to learn from other aspects of life and avoid excessive indulgence. Emulating nature's industrious creatures, we can engage in moderation and continuous effort.

Another peculiar yet effective practice for self-control is to wait a moment before eating. By pausing in front of our plate and chewing slowly, we can enhance mindfulness and develop self-discipline.

The goal of these exercises is to become familiar with hardship and become content with what we have. Self-control liberates us from the dependence on external factors for happiness. As Seneca puts it, it allows us to be "intimate with poverty," preparing us to face life's challenges with grace.

In summary, self-control is a powerful tool to avoid enslavement to desires and external influences. To nurture this virtue, we can experiment with abstinence, limit leisure time, and practice mindful eating. By embracing stoic wisdom, we can master self-control and find contentment in life's simplicity.

14

CULTIVATING SELF-CONFIDENCE WITH MARCUS AURELIUS - EMBRACING STOIC PRINCIPLES

The stoics held the belief that true happiness can only be achieved through virtuous actions, not external gains. In life, great achievements often demand boldness and perseverance, requiring us to face challenges and endure hardships. This courage is essential for creating something extraordinary, and it ultimately brings the most satisfaction.

Regardless of our position in society, life will inevitably call for us to take risks and bet on ourselves. This is where self-confidence plays a vital role. True self-confidence goes beyond mere words of affirmation or intellectual understanding; it comes from within and is shaped by our actions. To develop self-confidence, the stoics offer valuable advice:

Embrace Self-Acceptance: Recognize that self-confidence is intrinsically tied to self-acceptance. Embrace all aspects of yourself, including imperfections and shortcomings. Instead of running away from your dark side, acknowledge it and see it as an opportunity to grow and become a better person. Accept yourself unconditionally and love yourself, knowing that you are complete and whole as you are.

Take Ownership of Your Life: Empower yourself by taking responsibility for your choices and actions. Realize that you are the driving force behind your decisions and that you have the power to shape your life. Even in the face of obstacles, remember that your intentions remain within your control. Adapt and accommodate as needed, but always be the master of your destiny.

Stand Up for Your Beliefs: Authenticity and boldness go hand in hand. Be courageous enough to stand up for what you believe in, even if it means going against the crowd. Trust your intuition, that inner voice guiding you towards alignment with your values. Embrace your convictions and live them out, for they are the foundation of true self-confidence.

By following these stoic principles, you can build genuine self-confidence that allows you to write your own story and navigate life with courage and conviction. Remember, true self-confidence is not about seeking approval from others but finding strength from within and owning your journey.

So, what steps are you taking to nurture your self-confidence? As we've learned, self-confidence empowers you to shape your life, stand for your beliefs, and wholeheartedly accept yourself. By embodying these stoic principles, you can develop unwavering self-confidence and embrace life with purpose and resilience.

15

MASTERING INDIFFERENCE TO OTHERS' OPINIONS - INSIGHTS FROM MARCUS AURELIUS

An American sociologist once captured our irrational fixation on what others think, saying, 'I am not the person I think I am, and I am not who you think I am. I am who I think you think I am.' This peculiar obsession with external validation can be unproductive and even detrimental to our happiness. The stoics, led by Marcus Aurelius, offer timeless wisdom on how to care less about the opinions of others and find contentment within ourselves.

One powerful approach is to step into the mind of the 'judger.' Suppose someone is criticizing or judging you; Marcus Aurelius suggests understanding their perspective and assessing their character. Often, you'll find that these opinions hold no weight or value. Why should you strive to impress someone you don't respect or admire? By looking into the soul of the 'judger,' you'll realize that their opinions do not deserve the importance you've given them.

Consulting with logic is another effective way to cultivate indifference to others' opinions. Most of the time, the fear of disapproval is baseless, and seeking external validation is not necessary for survival or happiness. A good reputation, though preferable, is merely a 'preferred indifferent' for the stoics. Living a virtuous life and staying true to your principles are far more significant than seeking constant validation. Marcus Aurelius questioned the true value of public praise, likening it to the sound of clacking tongues—temporary pleasure that fails to bring lasting contentment.

Rather than allowing the opinions of others to dictate your actions and emotions, focus on what you can control. The more you attach value to uncontrollable factors, the less control you have over your life. Embrace indifference by understanding that others' opinions are beyond your influence. Instead, stay true to yourself, embrace self-acceptance, and make decisions based on logic and virtue, not the fleeting approval of others.

To care less about the opinions of others, follow the wisdom of the stoics:

Step into the mind of the 'judger' and recognize their opinions' insignificance.

Consult with logic and understand that external validation is not necessary for happiness.

By adopting these stoic principles, you can free yourself from the burden of seeking constant approval and find contentment within yourself. Remember, true self-confidence arises from embracing your authentic self and prioritizing your values over the fleeting judgments of others.

16

EMBRACING INNER FREEDOM: LEARNING FROM THE STOICS

In our materialistic and status-driven world, the Stoics' philosophy offers valuable insights into finding contentment and inner freedom. Marcus Aurelius and Epictetus emphasized the importance of detaching ourselves from external possessions and recognition. A common modern-day phenomenon called "lifestyle creep" can lead to financial and emotional distress as we endlessly pursue more.

The Stoics' wisdom encourages us to be "losers" in the modern sense, not in terms of status but in our indifference to fame, wealth, and power. Instead, we should focus on what truly matters and see material possessions as mere conveniences, not necessities. By not tethering our self-worth to external factors, we retain the power to make decisions based on virtue and integrity, regardless of circumstances.

To strengthen our resolve, the Stoics advise contemplating the mortality of our heroes or role models. By recognizing that even the greatest individuals faced mortality, we can break the illusion of grandiosity that material success often creates. This contemplation instills humility and reminds us that true virtue and character matter more than fleeting achievements or possessions.

The essence of caring less lies in embracing our inner citadel. We liberate ourselves from being controlled by external circumstances and instead find solace in our self-reflective, virtuous core. To achieve this inner freedom, the Stoics suggest:

Embracing the notion of being a "loser," not defined by material wealth or status.

Regularly meditating on the mortality of our heroes, understanding that all achievements are ephemeral.

Through these Stoic teachings, we can liberate ourselves from the never-ending pursuit of external validation and possessions. Instead, we find contentment by valuing virtue, integrity, and our inner selves.

17

LIBERATE YOURSELF FROM OTHERS' OPINIONS

Have you ever found yourself constrained by the fear of what others might think? In the past, relying on the opinions of others was essential for survival, ensuring social cohesion and safety. However, times have changed, and modern technology has connected us on a global scale. Despite this shift, our instinctual need for approval remains deeply ingrained.

To truly free ourselves, we must update our mental model of life. Epictetus emphasizes that genuine freedom comes from doing what we desire without being coerced or impeded by others. Trying to please everyone is futile, as everyone will have differing opinions. Instead, we should focus on our actions and bettering ourselves, unaffected by opposition or criticism.

Consider how much energy is wasted on caring about what others say. In truth, their opinions should not dictate our choices or define us. By concentrating on our actions, we can create our narrative, unaffected by external judgments. Inner peace comes when we stop giving mental space to others' thoughts and instead focus on our own path.

To liberate ourselves from the chains of others' opinions, we must:

Update our mental model for life, recognizing that true freedom lies in doing what we believe is right, irrespective of others' opinions.

Focus on our actions and let them speak for us, rather than getting caught up in seeking validation from others.

These steps can set us on a path of self-empowerment, freeing us from the burden of others' opinions. So, ask yourself, how free are you? Embrace your authenticity and prioritize your actions over the opinions of others to find true liberation and peace.

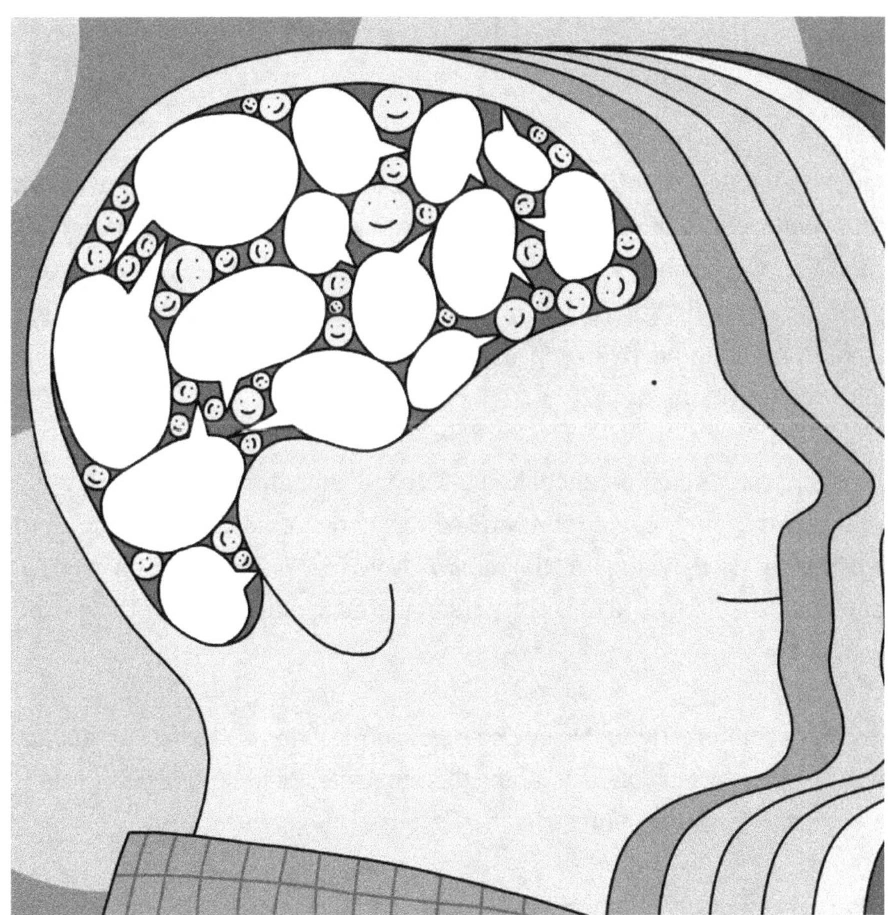

18

FREE YOURSELF FROM THE SHACKLES OF OTHERS' OPINIONS

As the stoics wisely pointed out, obsessing over what others think of us is a futile endeavor. Although it's natural to care about others' opinions, letting them dictate our choices or self-worth can harm our well-being and inner peace. Instead, finding confidence and happiness lies in seeking validation from within. Here are five compelling reasons from the stoics to stop worrying about others' opinions:

Intrinsic value remains unchanged: Others' thoughts about us are mere reflections of their perceptions and beliefs. Their opinions don't alter our true worth. Recognizing this liberates us from the stress of seeking external approval, enabling us to focus on personal growth and becoming the person we want to be.

Embrace your creativity: No one else can define who you are or hinder your creative expressions. Understanding this empowers us to explore our passions and talents fearlessly, unrestricted by external judgments.

Internal standards for success: While we should consider others' opinions selectively, our primary focus should be clarifying our goals and aspirations. With a clear path, the weight of external judgment lessens, allowing us to forge ahead confidently.

Unraveling others' baggage: Realize that others often project their insecurities and regrets onto us. Don't elevate their opinions to an unwarranted pedestal. Focus on verifiable facts and let go of unverifiable opinions.

Mastering your emotions: Taking charge of your feelings is essential. Don't relinquish control over your internal world to others. Instead, choose how to respond to their words, allowing room for learning and growth.

Remember, attaching self-worth to others' opinions leads to suffering and victimhood. Embrace the wisdom of the stoics, and liberate yourself from the chains of others' judgments. Let your actions, creativity, and internal standards define your journey, and reclaim control over your emotions. With these insights in mind, you'll pave the way to a more fulfilled and authentic life.

19

NAVIGATING THE JOURNEY OF HEALING AFTER A BREAKUP

At some point in our lives, we all experience the pain of a breakup. The depth of love we once shared now becomes tangled in conflicts, misunderstandings, or mistakes. So, how do we cope with the aftermath of a shattered relationship? The stoics offered valuable insights on healing from heartbreak, and their wisdom remains relevant even in our modern dating landscape.

Before we delve into their teachings, it's essential to understand why breakups hurt so much. Falling in love triggers a surge of chemicals that create euphoria and attachment. This "honeymoon phase" eventually gives way to a deeper emotional connection. When a breakup occurs, it disrupts this attachment and can leave us feeling lost. But the stoics believed that we could overcome this pain with the power of rational thinking.

Here are some beliefs the stoics encouraged us to change to ease the burden of a breakup:

Happiness does not solely depend on them: Stoicism challenges the idea that our happiness hinges on another person's presence. True joy comes from living a virtuous life, not from external factors like relationships. While the pain of a breakup is undeniable, redirecting focus to self-improvement can lead to greater happiness and fulfillment.

Embrace detachment: Recognize that love is a gift, not an entitlement. Stoics like Epictetus believed that love, like any gift, could be given and taken away. By viewing love as a returned gift, you release the sense of being wronged when a relationship ends.

Time heals all wounds: Although it may seem impossible to overcome heartbreak, time has a remarkable way of healing us. The passage of time reshapes our experiences and emotions, allowing us to process grief naturally. Embrace your feelings, let time do its work, and eventually, the pain will subside.

Grief requires patience: Like medicine, grief needs time to take its course before applying remedies. Allow yourself to cry, feel the pain, and acknowledge your emotions. Stoics like Seneca advised taking the time to let grief exhaust itself, making room for healing and growth.

As we grapple with the aftermath of a breakup, stoicism offers us solace and guidance. While the dating culture may have evolved, our emotions and human experiences remain rooted in the timeless nature of humanity. By applying the wisdom of the stoics, we can find resilience, healing, and a renewed sense of self-worth on the path to recovery.

20

EMBRACING STOIC WISDOM: OVERCOMING HEARTBREAK AND FINDING INNER PEACE

In the aftermath of a heartbreak, it's easy to fall into a spiral of pain and despair. However, Stoic philosophy offers invaluable insights on how to navigate these challenging times and emerge stronger than before.

One fundamental rule is to avoid exacerbating the situation. When you find yourself in a hole, stop digging. After a breakup, it's natural to feel hurt and angry, but reacting impulsively can only make things worse. Resist the urge to seek immediate distractions or place blame. Instead, choose to reflect on the positive aspects of the relationship and use it as an opportunity for personal growth.

Blaming others for the breakup only prolongs the suffering. Stoic thinker Epictetus advised against seeking scapegoats and encouraged taking responsibility for one's actions. Remember that life is divided into "dead time" and "alive time." Embrace the latter by actively learning, acting, and making the most of your moments.

In times of need, do not hesitate to seek help. There is no shame in asking for support during difficult times. Marcus Aurelius compared it to a soldier needing assistance on the battlefield. Surround yourself with a support network that can offer comfort and guidance.

Rather than dwelling on negative thoughts about the past or an uncertain future, focus on the present. Think of how you've overcome challenges in the past and use that strength to survive the current situation. By zooming in on the details of your life, you can avoid feeling overwhelmed by the bigger picture.

Perhaps the most radical Stoic advice for healing from heartbreak is to choose love over hate. While it may be tempting to harbor resentment or seek revenge, love is a powerful force that can heal wounds and lead to inner peace. Love those who have hurt you, love those who have rejected you, and let love guide your actions.

Heartbreak can be blinding, clouding our judgment and perspective. To break free from this loop of pain, embrace Stoic wisdom by changing your beliefs, not making things worse, taking responsibility, seeking help, focusing on the present, and always choosing love over hate. With these principles as your guide, you can emerge from heartbreak with newfound strength and wisdom.

21

EMBRACING EMOTIONAL RESILIENCE: HOW TO RISE ABOVE OFFENSE

The Stoics' wisdom teaches us that taking offense is a choice we make, and with conscious effort, we can cultivate emotional resilience to avoid being disturbed by others' actions. In a world filled with differing opinions and the allure of outrage, it is essential to equip ourselves with the Stoic principles to lead a happier life.

The first step in not getting offended is to depersonalize opinions. When someone expresses their views, remind yourself that it's not a personal attack. Opinions are shaped by individual experiences and values, and they may not reflect the objective truth. Instead of taking offense, engage in healthy debates without feeling attacked. Understand that differences in opinion are natural and respect the diversity of perspectives.

Accepting differences is key to avoiding offense. The outrage culture often leads to confrontational approaches that do more harm than good. Instead of trying to change others' opinions forcefully, cultivate understanding and empathy. Engage in thoughtful discussions, raising your arguments with kindness, rather than raising your voice with anger. Respect that you cannot control other people's beliefs, but you can control your reactions.

At the core of not getting offended lies self-mastery. When someone offends you, practice compassion, as Marcus Aurelius advised. Consider their perspective and see the difference in values between them and yourself. Respond with kindness and avoid harboring malice. Your strength lies in being invincible with kindness, rather than succumbing to offense.

Mastering yourself means acting rightly regardless of how others treat you. If someone behaves poorly, it is their responsibility to see their actions, not yours. Focus on your own actions, choosing kindness and integrity over taking offense. This self-management and integrity serve as an antidote to the toxicity of offense.

In the face of potential offense, remember that it is a choice you make. By mastering yourself, you gain control over your emotions and reactions. Choose not to be upset and find compassion for those who may offend you. Let others' actions be their concern, while you focus on acting rightly with kindness.

In conclusion, Stoicism provides valuable insights on how to rise above offense and foster emotional resilience. Remember that other people's opinions are not personal attacks but expressions of their values. Accept that disagreements are part of life and respect others' perspectives. Choose compassion over outrage, and practice self-mastery by responding with kindness and integrity. By embracing these Stoic principles, you can navigate through life's challenges with greater equanimity and happiness.

22

THREE STOIC APPROACHES TO EMBRACING LETTING GO

'A philosopher expects all hurt and benefit from himself. A proficient one censures no one, accuses no one, praises no one, and blames no one.' – Epictetus

In previous discussions, we emphasized the importance of learning to let go to find inner peace. However, the question remains: how do we truly let go? Stoic wisdom offers three practical exercises and insights into the workings of the world that can lead us to a happier life. These include:

Reevaluate your judgments

According to the Stoics, events and circumstances themselves do not possess inherent goodness or badness. It is our own minds that assign value to them. By recognizing this, we gain the power to control our judgments. Epictetus argued that our experiences affect us based on how we judge them. By cultivating a mindset that aligns with nature, we can achieve a happier existence. It is essential to be mindful of our judgments, especially regarding things beyond our control.

Embrace virtuous living

Stoic ethics place great emphasis on virtues and vices, guiding us to live in harmony with nature. Virtue, aligned with nature, leads to happiness. To learn the art of letting go, practice wisdom, moderation, courage, and justice in your daily life. When faced with ambiguous situations, apply the pursuit of virtue to make wise choices. Living virtuously empowers us to release attachments and find tranquility within.

Lower your expectations

Excessively high expectations set us up for disappointment, especially when directed towards things beyond our control. If we expect others to behave in specific ways and they do not, we end up feeling let down. Epictetus reminds us that we are not entitled to the fulfillment of every desire, but only to what is naturally ours. When we expect more than what nature offers, we inflict suffering upon ourselves. Marcus Aurelius, too, recognized the value of tempering expectations. Preparing himself for the day, he anticipated the challenges of encountering disloyalty, ingratitude, and selfishness from others. By adjusting our expectations, we can navigate life's uncertainties with greater serenity.

What burdens are you carrying that are not yours to bear? What attachments are causing you emotional pain? Stoicism provides a path to let go by:

Managing your expectations,

Embracing virtuous living.

Reevaluating your judgments of events and the world.

Through these practices, we can cultivate emotional resilience, achieve inner freedom, and embrace a more contented life.

23

STRENGTHENING YOUR MENTAL RESOLVE: STOIC PRACTICES

'You have power over your mind – not outside events. Realize this, and you will find strength.' – Marcus Aurelius

Have you ever found yourself doubting your capabilities or feeling inadequate in life? Are worries and concerns overwhelming you, weighing you down with their burdens? Do you often second-guess your decisions? If you can relate to any of these experiences, you might be struggling with a weak mental resolve. The solution lies in stepping out of your comfort zone and working on building mental strength.

Mental toughness empowers individuals to confront and overcome doubts, worries, and challenges that hinder success. It acts as a fortress against setbacks, allowing you to face fears and uncertainties head-on. This resilience is not limited to athletes; it applies to anyone striving for greatness. History has shown that truly exceptional individuals persevere when others falter, holding firm to their convictions even in the face of adversity.

True greatness goes beyond societal notions of success; it is the ability to triumph over the challenges and disasters that life throws our way. Seneca eloquently puts it that success may come to those with little talent, but greatness lies in conquering the panics and disasters that life presents. To rise above mediocrity and embrace genuine success, we must cultivate the endurance to stay the course, endure rejection, and embrace learning through difficult times. There are no shortcuts to mental toughness; it is earned through overcoming obstacles and adversity.

The Stoics, recognizing the incalculable value of mental strength, offer wisdom to foster greater resilience, including:

Cultivate Resourcefulness

Epictetus understood the limitations of giving generalized advice. He believed that true strength lies in training the mind to be adaptable. In a constantly changing world, rigidity and inflexibility prove detrimental. The ability to handle ambiguity and navigate through unforeseen challenges becomes vital. Life rarely adheres to a structured plan; it demands resourcefulness and adaptability. Embrace the uncertainties and be prepared to forge your own path, leveraging your life experiences to thrive in any circumstance.

Embrace Solitude

Seneca recognized that a well-ordered mind is marked by the ability to pause plans and spend time alone. Solitude fosters introspection, enabling us to discover what truly matters and set our life's direction. By dedicating time to introspection, we connect with ourselves and attain a state of focused productivity, the elusive state of "flow." Prioritize spending time alone, and you will cultivate stability and resilience.

Create More, Consume Less

Sustained immersion in a field of study or pursuit requires dedication and commitment. It demands resilience to persist even when faced with monotony and challenges. Some may shy away from such commitments, opting for distractions and illusions. However, true mental strength lies in honoring your vision and seeing your endeavors through to fruition. Whether building a business, creating art, or mastering any craft, the commitment to persevere defines your character and shapes your legacy.

To build mental strength, contemplate these Stoic practices:

- Spend time alone for introspection.
- Cultivate resourcefulness in adapting to life's challenges.
- Create more than you consume and persist in your pursuits.

Through these Stoic principles, you can enhance your mental toughness, overcome obstacles, and lead a purposeful, resilient life.

24

RELEASE AND FLOURISH: STOIC PRACTICES FOR MENTAL TOUGHNESS

'It is not insults or ill language that is insulting, but the principle interpreting them. When anyone provokes you, be assured that it is your own opinion that provokes you.' – Epictetus

Epictetus, the ancient Stoic philosopher, observed that our burdens in life often stem from caring too much about things that don't truly matter. He encouraged us to care less about trivial matters and focus only on what is genuinely important. But determining what truly matters can be challenging, as it is influenced by our ever-changing perceptions of the world. Nevertheless, there are aspects of life we can change, and others that are beyond our control. Mental toughness is about discerning when to let go and when to hold on, and Epictetus provides valuable guidance on how to achieve this:

Release Attachment to Borrowed Goods

Attachments to people and material possessions can lead to immense pain when we fear their loss or cling to their presence. We must understand that everything in life is transient, much like guests at a dinner party. We should welcome them with open arms when they arrive and bid them farewell when they depart, gracefully acknowledging that life's impermanence is the essence of its beauty. Clinging to borrowed goods, such as relationships and power, only exposes us to suffering when they are inevitably taken away. Adopting a mindset of non-attachment allows us to appreciate the time we have with people and possessions while they are present, freeing us from unnecessary pain.

Release the Need for Others' Approval

In today's hyper-connected world, many seek validation and approval from others. However, Epictetus reminds us that true equanimity should never be at the mercy of external factors, including the opinions of others. While being liked by others may have its benefits, it should not govern our inner peace. The pursuit of being liked can be exhausting and compromise our tranquility. Embracing ridicule and being despised by some may be the price we pay for true serenity, freedom, and inner balance. We cannot control other people's opinions, but we can choose how they affect us. Releasing the need for constant approval liberates us from the constraints of others' judgments.

Release Attachment to Fixed Ideas and Outcomes

Life becomes burdensome when we resist the reality of what is and endlessly pursue what we believe should be. Epictetus uses the analogy of a servant who should obey but not be expected to follow every command. Similarly, we must learn to accept that people and circumstances will not always conform to our expectations. Instead of trying to control the world, we should focus on controlling ourselves and our reactions. Embracing life as it is, while being kind to ourselves and others, enables us to navigate its ups and downs with strength and resilience. By relinquishing attachment to fixed outcomes, we free ourselves from unnecessary suffering and allow ourselves to flourish.

In essence, Epictetus teaches us the art of letting go. By detaching ourselves from:

- Fixed ideas and outcomes,
- The opinions of others, and
- The illusion of ownership over borrowed goods,

We can achieve mental toughness, live with greater equanimity, and embrace life's uncertainties with resilience and grace.

25

FORTIFY YOUR MIND: EMBRACING STOIC MENTAL TOUGHNESS

'When you arise in the morning, think what a precious privilege it is to be alive – to breathe, to think, to enjoy, to love.' – Marcus Aurelius

Sometimes, people confuse fortitude with isolation, seeking refuge in physical separation from the world's challenges. However, true strength lies not in self-isolation but in fortifying our mental faculties to navigate life's difficulties and adversities. The Stoics advocated for this approach, emphasizing the importance of building mental fortitude to lead a fulfilling life. By following some key Stoic principles, we can cultivate the strength of mind to face life head-on and embrace its uncertainties:

Examine Your Beliefs About Life

Our beliefs profoundly influence how we experience life, and often, it is our own beliefs that cause us pain and suffering. Instead of connecting our happiness to specific expectations that may go unfulfilled, we should strive to adopt a more accepting perspective. Seneca wisely pointed out that it is not life itself but our beliefs that bring us distress. By acknowledging the reality that life includes both benevolent and malevolent elements, we can approach it with a peaceful mindset. Embracing the inevitability of death also fosters mental fortitude, as it reminds us to live each day fully without being surprised by life's unpredictable nature.

Curb Your Aversions and Desires

Mental fortitude is built on restraining our aversions and desires. Epictetus urged us to defer desire and direct our aversion only towards things we can control. When our moods depend on uncontrollable external factors, our stability becomes precarious. Cultivating indifference toward things beyond our control is key to mental strength. This means not seeking excessive praise, approval, or possessions and focusing instead on our actions and responses to life's challenges.

Do Only Good

Chrysippus, an esteemed Stoic philosopher, emphasized that all our actions should aim at living a happy life. To achieve this, we must discern what is truly good and virtuous and act accordingly. Doing good often requires courage, as it may involve facing fears and confronting pain. While vice promises fleeting pleasure, choosing virtue may lead to temporary discomfort but ultimately brings lasting satisfaction and a sense of fulfillment. By cultivating the courage to resist vice and pursue goodness, we become stronger in the face of adversity and maintain control over our choices.

In summary, Stoic mental fortitude involves:

- Letting go of rigid expectations and accepting life as it is.
- Cultivating indifference toward external factors beyond our control.
- Displaying courage to act virtuously and do good despite challenges.

By embracing these principles, we can build mental resilience and lead a more content and purposeful life.

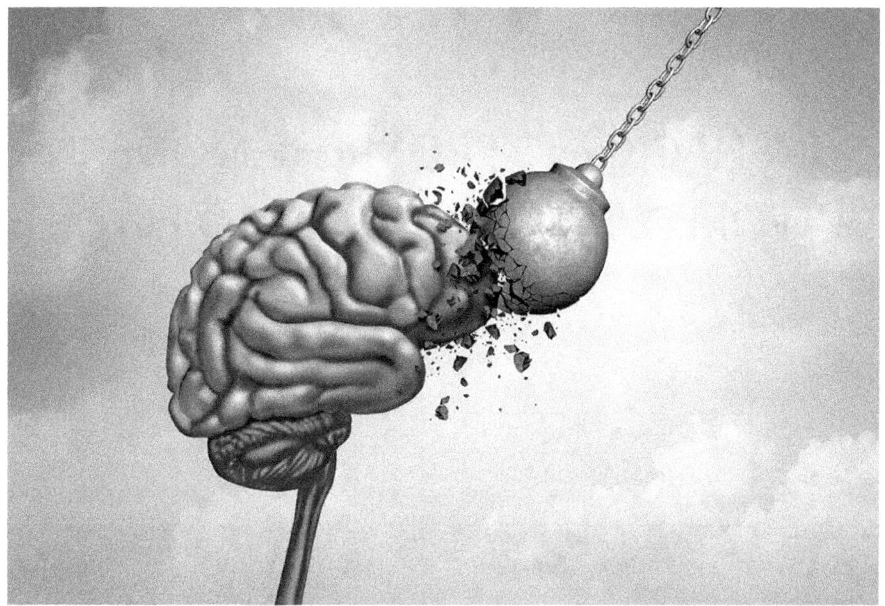

26

UNSHACKLING FROM THE MODERN WORLD: STOIC WISDOM TO FIND FREEDOM

'If all geniuses in history focused on this one theme, they could never fully explain how baffled they are by the human mind. No one would surrender their estate and *the smallest dispute with a neighbor would breed chaos; yet, very easily, we allow others to encroach our lives. Worse, we create the way for them to take over. No one gives their money to a passerby, but how often do we hand over our lives to others! We hold on to our money and property and think little of wasting time, the one thing we should all be miserly about.' – Seneca*

While we may not be literal slaves like Epictetus, the modern world presents its own chains that bind us. These chains are not specific religious, cultural, or political systems, but rather the invisible constraints of our environment. The decisions we make seem to be dictated by everything around us, leaving us vulnerable to manipulation by external forces. We become slaves to our desires and dislikes, controlled by fear, blame, and shame. From corporations to political parties, anyone can take advantage of our susceptibility as long as they offer something we crave. To find true freedom, we must embrace Stoic wisdom, which offers insights to break these chains. Here are five Stoic ideas that can liberate us from the modern world's grip:

Premeditate the worst – Premeditation Malorum

Seneca suggests premeditating the worst-case scenarios to prepare for setbacks and uncertainties that life inevitably brings. By envisioning possible misfortunes and losses, we build resilience and reduce the impact of unexpected events. By training ourselves to project our thoughts ahead, we can be ready to face any fate.

Meditate on the mutual interdependence of all things

The Stoics believed in the interconnectedness of all things in the universe. By understanding our unity with others and the world, we can empathize, make fair judgments, and reduce divisions among races and people. Adopting a higher perspective, known as 'sympatheia,' helps us challenge our preconceptions and see life more accurately.

Remember the highest good

According to Marcus Aurelius, the highest good in life lies in truth, justice, self-control, and courage, which collectively constitute virtue. Pursuing virtue leads to a meaningful and fulfilling life, even if it challenges societal norms or goes unrecognized by others.

The ego is the enemy

Stoics warn against ego-driven self-deception and delusions of grandeur, which hinder growth, learning, and progress. The ego blinds us to truth and undermines empathy, vulnerability, and teamwork. Letting go of ego and embracing humility enables genuine growth and self-improvement.

Embrace the Stoic philosophy to find liberation from the chains imposed by the modern world. By premeditating the worst, recognizing our interconnectedness, pursuing virtue, and shedding our egos, we can attain true freedom and live life on our own terms.

Overcoming the Chains of the Modern World: Stoic Wisdom for True Liberation

Epictetus believed that if you already assume you know everything, learning becomes impossible. The ego hinders growth, improvement, and the respect of others. When you see yourself as perfect, you become an enemy to the person you aspire to be. The Stoics advised confronting the ego with contempt and hostility, keeping it at bay day by day. By avoiding ego-driven behavior, you increase your chances of success significantly.

Memento Mori - Remember Death

In Silicon Valley, there's a buzz about achieving immortality and merging with artificial intelligence. Some fear death so much that they avoid thinking about it. However, true wisdom lies in embracing death and living accordingly. Seneca urged us to prepare our minds for death, living each day as though it were our last. The Romans reminded victorious leaders of their mortality during celebrations, to prevent delusions of grandeur.

Living each day as if it were your last is more than a cliché; it's about mindful living. Stoics understood that life and thoughtfulness are inseparable. To break free from the modern world's chains, you must:

- Pre-meditate the worst.
- Recognize the interconnectedness of all things.
- Pursue the highest good.
- Abandon the ego.
- Remember death.

By following these Stoic principles, you can find true liberation from the constraints of the modern world and live a purposeful and meaningful life.

9 783988 316196